9.50

GRASSLANDS

THIS EARTH OF OURS

Mel Higginson

The Rourke Corporation, Inc.
Vero Beach, Florida 32964

Edited by Sandra A. Robinson

PHOTO CREDITS
© Mel Higginson: cover, title page, pages 4, 7, 8, 10, 12, 13,
15, 21; © Frank Balthis: page 17; © James P. Rowan: page 18

Library of Congress Cataloging-in-Publication Data

Higginson, Mel, 1942-
    Grasslands / by Mel Higginson.
        p. cm. — (This earth of ours)
    Includes index.
    ISBN 0-86593-381-2
    1. Grassland ecology—Juvenile literature. 2. Grasslands—
Juvenile literature. [1. Grassland ecology. 2. Ecology.] I. Title.
II. Series: Higginson, Mel, 1942-   This earth of ours.
QH541.5.P7H53   1994
574.5'264—dc20   94-9402
                                                          CIP
                                                          AC
Printed in the USA

TABLE OF CONTENTS

GRASSLANDS

Here and there throughout the world are huge patches of naturally grassy land. Instead of being covered by trees or desert plants, grasslands are covered mostly by wild grasses.

In North America, grasslands are often called prairies. European grasslands are called steppes. In South America, the pampas are grasslands.

Some of the wild grasslands that remain today are **habitats,** or homes, to large numbers of animals. Millions of hoofed animals still graze Africa's grasslands.

Great herds of wildebeests and other hoofed animals graze Africa's grasslands

WHERE GRASSLANDS ARE

Grasslands usually lie between deserts, which are dry, and forests, which are fairly moist. In North America, the western states and **provinces** have large grasslands.

Grasslands are also in parts of Africa, Asia, Europe and South America. One of the best-known grasslands is the **savanna** of East Africa. Savannas are grasslands with clumps, or small groups, of trees. East Africa's savannas are famous for their herds of antelopes, elephants, zebras and other grazing animals.

A termite mound (left) rises from an East African savanna where a herd of elephants roams

LIFE OF THE GRASSLANDS

Grasslands support a wide range of plant and animal life. Many kinds of plants — not just grasses — grow in these wild "pastures."

America's grasslands are homes for grass-eating prairie dogs, pronghorns and small herds of bison. Badgers, snakes, grasshoppers, falcons and dozens of other kinds of animals live there, too.

In Africa, the great herds of grass-eaters are trailed by cheetahs, lions, leopards, hyenas, **jackals** and wild dogs.

Prairie dogs, a kind of ground squirrel, live on the western prairies of North America

9

HOW ANIMALS LIVE IN THE GRASSLANDS

Animals have special ways to survive in the grasslands. Many, for example, are good runners. Grasslands are open and fairly flat. Being able to run — rather than climb — is useful to grassland animals. North American pronghorns can race at nearly 60 miles per hour to escape from **predators,** the animals that hunt them.

The pronghorn is one of the fastest grassland runners, but it is not as fast as the cheetah. Cheetahs dash at nearly 70 miles per hour to catch **prey** in Africa.

Panting, a pair of cheetahs rest after bringing down a wildebeest calf in Kenya

A young lion on the Serengeti Plains chases vultures from its kill

North America's moist, easternmost prairies have thick, tall grasses

A GRASSLANDS ANIMAL: THE AMERICAN BISON

American bison are perfectly fit for life on the prairies. They are grazing animals, so the prairie grasses are an endless meal.

For protection from predators, a bison has speed, horns and bulk. No predator, by itself, is big or fast enough to kill a healthy bison bull.

For protection from cold prairie winters, a bison has thick, shaggy hair.

An American bison bull bellows on a South Dakota prairie

PEOPLE IN THE GRASSLANDS

Much of the prairie land in North America and elsewhere has been plowed and planted. Many American and Canadian farmers live on land that was prairie long ago.

Before the American Civil War (1861-1865), the North American prairies were the homes of Plains Indians — Sioux, Arapaho, Blackfeet and others. They lived in tepee homes made of bison skins.

In East Africa, some of the Masai people still live on the savannas.

Masai tribespeople of East Africa's savannas show off traditional crafts and weapons

HOW PEOPLE LIVE ON THE GRASSLANDS

When Native Americans lived on the North American prairies, they followed the herds of bison. Millions of bison provided the Plains tribes with most of the things they needed to live. Bison meat was food. Bison skins and furry coats were used for tepees and clothing. Bison **dung,** or waste, was dried and burned for fuel.

The Masai of the African grasslands are cattle and goat herders. Their animals fill many of their needs, too.

A bison skull and tepee are reminders of the American Plains Indians

THE GRASSLANDS COMMUNITY

The plants and animals of the grasslands survive in their world together. Each member of this natural community takes something and gives something.

The heart of the community is grass. Its roots hold the soil, and its blades feed a great many animals, large and small.

The grass and other plants live by making food from sunshine and soil. Animals like antelopes live by eating plants. Others, such as the lion and falcon, live by hunting plant-eaters.

An African leopard pauses by its prize, a grass-eating topi antelope

A GRASSLANDS COMMUNITY: THE SERENGETI

The Serengeti Plains of East Africa is one of the world's last great grasslands. Rich soil and **seasonal** rains keep the Serengeti grasses healthy. These grasses feed the largest herds of grazing animals on Earth — zebras, **wildebeests,** gazelles, impalas and elephants.

With so many grazing animals, the Serengeti is a paradise for predators. When a lion or cheetah finishes its meal, vultures and hyenas feed noisily on the remains. Nothing in the grassland community is wasted.

Glossary

dung (DUNG) — the solid waste of an animal

habitat (HAB uh tat) — the special kind of area where an animal or plant lives, such as *grassland*

jackal (JAH kul) — a small, long-legged wild dog of Africa and Asia

predator (PRED uh tor) — an animal that kills other animals for food

prey (PRAY) — an animal killed by another animal for food

province (PRAH vihnts) — one of several, separate regions or divisions of Canada, each of which has a provincial government

savanna (suh VAN nuh) — broad, grassy lands with clumps, or small groups, of trees

seasonal (SEEZ un ul) — happening during a particular season

wildebeest (WIHLD eh beest) — an African antelope that lives and travels in large herds

INDEX